Marriage 101 Mini-Series

COMMUNICATION

Jewell R. Powell

Marriage 101 Mini-Series: Communication

ISBN: 978-0-9745528-5-9

Unless otherwise indicated, all scripture quotations are taken from the King James Version (KJV) of the Bible.

Scripture taken from THE AMPLIFIED BIBLE, Old Testament, Copyright © 1965, 1987 by the Zondervan Corporation. The Amplified New Testament, copyright © 1958, 1987 by the Lockman Foundation. Used by permission. Amplified Bible (AB). 1.C.

Scripture taken from the HOLY BIBLE, NEW INTERNATIONAL VERSION®, copyright © 1973, 1978, 1984 by International Bible Society. Used by permission of Zondervan Publishing House. All rights reserved.

The NIV and New International Version trademarks are registered in the United States Patent and Trademark Office by International Bible Society. Use of either trademark requires the permission of International Bible Society.

Scripture taken from THE MESSAGE, copyright © 1993, 1994, 1995, 1996, 2000, 2001, 2002. Used by permission of NavPress Publishing Group.

Scripture taken from the New American Standard Bible®, copyright © 1960, 1962, 1963, 1968, 1971, 1972, 1973, 1975, 1977, 1995 by the Lockman Foundation. Used by permission.

NOTE: Jokes were taken from the following website: http://www.romancestuck.com/jokes/marriage-jokes.htm

If you have testimonies or comments on any material in this book, please email them to info@marriage101.us.

Cover Design: Laurie Fenner

Table of Contents

While attending a Marriage Seminar dealing with communication, Tom and his wife Grace listened to the instructor, "It is essential that husbands and wives know each other's likes and dislikes." He addressed the man, "Can you name your wife's favorite flower?" Tom leaned over, touched his wife's arm gently and whispered, "It's Pillsbury, isn't it?" He addressed the woman, "Can you describe your husband's favorite sport?" She said, "Sex."

Communication among couples can be vastly complicated by the mind games we learn to play through the years. However, if we are going to develop healthy communication with our spouses, we need to shed those bad habits and learn how to communicate effectively with our spouses. It doesn't make sense to play games when we can truly connect with each other and develop deeper relationships that can stand the test of time.

It takes time and patience to develop effective communication, especially with those of the opposite sex. It is as if we don't speak the same language; however, when we speak kindly and lovingly towards one another it's a great start.

Remember that we are encouraged in the Bible to speak plainly and truthfully - *"Instead, speaking the truth in love, we will in all things grow up into Him who is the Head, that is, Christ."* (Eph 4:15 NIV)

It is imperative that we speak clearly and honestly to our spouses and children. People should not have to question or guess what you are trying to say. We should be honest in the sense that we should speak directly instead of using manipulation tactics. For example, if you want your husband to stop on the way home from work to pick up dinner, you don't need to build an elaborate, dramatic scheme to manipulate him to do it. Simply say something like, 'I've had a really busy day. Would you mind picking up dinner on the way home?'

Having a great marriage is not based on not having conflicts but learning how to resolve them. Effective communication is the transfer of information from one person (the sender) to another (the receiver) and how it is perceived by the receiver. One study shows that communication is 7% of what you say (words); 38% of how you say it (volume, pitch, rhythm); and 55% body language (facial expression, posture, etc.) (Source: A. Barbour, "Louder Than Words: Non-verbal Communication."). Moreover, we must remember it is a skill and we must develop the skill, especially when it comes to understanding our spouses. We automatically think someone should understand us because of what we said. Yes, we know how to talk but we must learn how to communicate in a way that others understand us. It is not their job to understand us but our responsibility to develop skills that will help us communicate more effectively to anyone we talk too.

When you have a breakdown in communication there will be conflict. There are many keys to developing effective communication. However, the core of effective communication is to examine yourself consistently as to what drives you (i.e. fear, pride, selfishness, etc.) and to make sure you are respectful to others (speaking kindly, keeping emotions under control, etc.). For example, do you have to win every argument (prideful)? Or, are your cursing and yelling because your emotions are out of control?

Remember, God is always trying to teach us a lesson (usually it is one of the fruit of the Spirit-see Galatians 5:22-23) so we can learn and grow spiritually. Ask yourself in each situation, "What is God trying to teach me?"

Key #1

―――∽⊙⒎⒎⒡⒡⒡⒡∽―――

The Art of Listening

―――∽⒎⒎⒡⒡⒡⒡∽―――

"My dear brothers (and sisters), take note of this: Everyone should be quick to listen, slow to speak and slow to become angry," (James 1:19 NIV)

God gave us two ears and only one mouth for a reason. How many of us have heard that one too many times? However, sadly it is often forgotten in the heat of an argument or in the midst of an entangling discussion. Even when you are listening to what your spouse is saying, the thought processes that are taking place in your mind may be working against your ability to truly be a good listener, and thus becoming a good communicator.

The art of listening involves more than simply gluing your lips shut long enough for the other person to finish a sentence. This type of listening is even referred to as combative or competitive listening. Not many counselors would encourage any activity referred to as "combative" when trying to maintain a loving and peace-filled home. The combative approach to communication is allowing the other person to speak, but all the while thinking of your response or rebuttal. In this way, your listening is compromised.

With all the internal dialogue going on in your head, even though you aren't speaking out loud, you are still listening to your own voice and thoughts while the other person is speaking. You can't really listen to two people at once with any kind of accuracy. To formulate your response in your head is truly to ignore a portion of what your spouse or child is trying to tell you. This is the best-case scenario. Let's face it; there are even times when we are simply waiting for a chance to take the floor of the discussion. Combative listening will never yield true communication.

During combative communication, we often overlook facial cues that can clarify statements that could otherwise be misconstrued. It is easier to determine a person's intent if you make an active choice to silence your internal dialogue. Refusing to listen to your own thoughts while another person is speaking will give them your exclusive attention. Not only does this improve your ability to hear what they are saying, but you can often discern what they are NOT saying as well.

Perhaps your husband is not saying he feels disrespected, but with discernment from the Holy Spirit and silencing your own internal voice, you can detect that feeling from his nonverbal signals. In that case, his feelings of disrespect or dishonor can be addressed and dealt with effectively. This information is valuable and could easily be overlooked had you been formulating a response versus silently listening to his words, as well as his heart.

Refraining from internal dialogue will also give value to the speaker. When you are speaking, you can tell if your listener is distracted or not completely engaged in what you are saying. Without voicing it, you feel a bit rejected and devalued. At the heart of good communication is respect for the other person involved. When someone feels as if their point of view or feelings have been valued, they are more likely to return that respect when listening to you. Honor goes a long way in maintaining healthy communication inside and outside the home.

Not only should you listen without formulating a response, but attempt to understand the person's point of view. Passive listening is silencing yourself long enough to truly hear what the other person is saying. Although it does give honor to the person who is speaking and increases your ability to pick up on facial cues and body language, active listening takes it a step farther. Active listening truly takes another positive stride toward effectively understanding the other person's point of view.

Active listening involves initially remaining silent while the other person is speaking. Then after your spouse (or another person) is done speaking, you weigh all the verbal and nonverbal communication and repeat back to the speaker what was said. In this way, misunderstandings and misattributed motives can be squashed before they ever begin.

It is also very helpful to use friendly phrases. Rather than say, "So, you mean to tell me, you've always hated my mother," try rephrasing it in a personal statement. For example, the previous statement could be reworded as, "What I hear you saying is that my mother makes you feel uncomfortable in your own home, and that you have begun to resent her for it." Rephrasing the "clarifying" question in a non-combative tone will also go a long way toward really hearing the person and valuing them as a child of God. Just remember, you're not on the defensive side of the discussion but you are a team working on how to communicate effectively and resolve the issue at hand.

The way people usually respond to others is based on the following: clichés, facts, opinions, beliefs, emotions, and even sarcasm. Effective listening will not only allow you to determine which way your spouse (or child) communicates, but can help you in determining how you should respond to them.

For example, if your preteen daughter comes to you because a boy at school told her she was fat, she will more than likely be communicating from an emotional level. If you listen silently, you will be able to hear what she is saying and respond at the level of communication she finds valuable. You will not respond with questions about the facts (the boy's name, the place, the verbatim break down of the insult), but rather you will respond on the level that you detected as valuable during your silent, respectful listening time. You will reply with, "I am so sorry your feelings are hurt. I too know what it is like to be made fun of, and it really hurts," or something of that nature.

It is unnecessary to continually ask yourself on what level the other person is talking while they are actually speaking. This would be additional internal dialogue, and the goal is to refrain from our own opinions, thoughts and feelings, at least while someone else is speaking. The level of communication will be easily perceived, just like the verbal and nonverbal communication. You will simply be able to discern what is of value to the speaker, if you value them by listening with your mind and heart, instead of just your ears.

Without pausing from our own thoughts and agendas, we will fail to hear what our loved ones are saying and on what level they are communicating with us. Many conflicts can be avoided by just listening, clarifying what was heard and responding to what was said and what wasn't on the level it was communicated.

Trying to come up with a winning argument while your spouse is bearing his or her soul will not lead to the peace and security we all truly long for. To make such a grievous oversight is disrespectful and counterproductive to healthy communication. Our goal is not to win the argument but to listen effectively to what is being said, respond in love and resolve the issue.

Key #2

Speak Kindly Towards Each Other

*"Kind words are like honey sweet to the soul and
healthy for the body." (Proverbs 16:24 NLT)*

A big part of seeing a vision bear fruit is choosing words
that uphold the vision in a positive light. There have been
numerous studies researching the power of words. Positive
words can also have health benefits for the speaker. People
who regularly speak encouraging words about themselves
and to others have less of a risk of depression and fewer
sick days at work.

Again Proverbs 16:24 in the NIV states that, *"Pleasant words
are a honeycomb, sweet to the soul and healing to the bones."*
It is not mystical or cultic to see the value in well-chosen
words. The words we speak can change our thinking and
the thoughts of those around us. Thoughts and beliefs can
then feed into the decisions we make. Our decisions in
turn seriously affect our current and future reality. It is our
responsibility to choose words that are negative or positive,
creating a desirable environment or destroying all things
we hope for.

Sharing a vision within a marriage has a lot to do with
encouraging the "vision sharer" when he or she loses sight
of the mutual goal. Realizing the value that words have
gives the encouraging spouse greater confidence in speaking

positive life into the heart of the discouraged one. When we stand in agreement many petty things fade into the shadows, but if we stand in disagreement, we will surely fall. Agreeing on future goals and speaking positive words into those goals have immeasurable worth in the happiness and longevity of a marriage, or any relationship for that matter.

With words being so valuable, the words we speak to our spouse are of vital importance to the health of the marriage. Our mouths can be a constant source of great power and inspiration, or they can be our own worst enemy. As one would expect, the more often wives and husbands speak encouraging words and voice agreement, the stronger the marriage is and the stronger it is likely to become in the future. Many factors need to be examined to lay a strong framework for this verbal agreement to come about and to remain strong for the life of the marriage.

First and foremost, each spouse needs to agree that the words they speak to one another should be respectful, uplifting, and comforting. Whether talkative or shy, eloquent or stuttering, each spouse needs to acknowledge the power of words. The reason this is so vital, is that as humans we honor what we find powerful. We will treat words carelessly if we underestimate the damage or the good that they are capable of. Many harsh words would go unsaid and many complements given if we would just realize the creative power of the words we choose to speak or to withhold. There is little hope for good communication if neither spouse acknowledges the importance of the words they share.

This decision to value words is better made on "sunny" days. In the heat of an argument, the ground rules should already be set. If the content of our character is deeply ingrained, we are far less likely to be someone different when we are angry. Sit down with your husband or wife and commit to honor the place words have in the home. If you jointly agree to revere words when you are getting along, you both are more likely to refrain from mishandling your words when you are angry.

James 1:26 (NLT) tells us, *"If you claim to be religious (Christians – my addition) but don't control your tongue, you are fooling yourself, and your religion is worthless."* We, as Christians, must learn how to tame our tongues. Choose a day that all is going well, and you both are getting along. On that day set ground rules for acceptable speech and how to rightly value words, both spoken and withheld. You will then have a better chance of respecting each other with what you speak in the moments you aren't getting along and everything is going poorly.

Moreover, is not just about controlling your tongue but also knowing how to respond. Whether you want to stop an argument or prevent one from happening, the key is *"a gentle answer deflects anger, but harsh words make tempers flare"* (Prov. 15:1 NLT). If you are anything like Lewis and me, we are very passionate, aggressive individuals. Our arguments use to tear the roof off the house and our children constantly asked us if we were getting a divorce. I've learned to ask the Holy Spirit to give me that gentle answer, especially during our heated discussions. Sometimes He would tell me to just shut up or ask if I could be excused, which leads me to my next point.

You and your spouse should also discuss some boundaries such as what you should do when a discussion becomes heated. For example, when Lewis and I would argue, I would just walk away. However, Lewis would follow me still arguing and cursing. I'm sure he must have had all kinds of feelings when I did that, such as, feeling disrespected, not being heard, or upset that the problem had not been solved. For me, I just needed time to calm down or else I would fall into the trap and get entangled with speaking negatively (OK, cursing him out) because he was cursing me out. Now, since we've sat down and discussed why I walked away, he understands and he gives me the space I need. We resume our discussion once we are in a better place to continue with better attitudes.

For some women, our mouths get us into a lot of trouble - our words can be lethal. When God revealed how nasty my mouth was and how disrespectfully I spoke to my husband, I had to change. Reading Proverbs 31 changed me, especially verse 26, *"She opens her mouth with wisdom, and on her tongue is the law of kindness."* I've realize that the only time I should open my mouth is when I have something worthwhile to say and to do it with kind words, not just to my spouse but to all people. Just that one little thing made such a significant impact in my marriage.

In summary, words are very powerful: they can build someone up or tear them down; they can bring joy or pain; they can respect or disrespect; stop an argument or start one – it's your choice. Using positive and encouraging words is an excellent way to build up a marriage to stand strong when the inevitable problems of conflict come up.

Key #3

Making Eye Contact

*"My bride, you have stolen my heart with one glance
of your eyes." (Song of Solomon 4:9a NIVR)*

Often, the success of a conversation can be determined
more by what is not said rather than what is voiced.
Physical cues and facial expressions can reveal more about
the listener or speaker than the words they choose. Eye
contact, in particular, can express interest or lack thereof.
How well a listener keeps the speaker's gaze can determine
how valued the speaker feels. It is perceived that where the
listener looks is where their attention lies. In contrast, if a
speaker diverts their gaze, it is sometimes interpreted as
dishonest communication by the listener. The importance
of maintaining eye contact is a healthy communication
lesson to learn.

In many cultures, keeping eye contact can be seen as
argumentative and abrupt, however in the United States
avoiding eye contact can be viewed as deceptive behavior.
At the very least, avoiding eye contact makes the listener
seem disinterested in what the speaker is saying. In the
worst case scenario, a speaker who refuses to maintain a
healthy eye-to-eye gaze is thought to be telling lies.

This perception has led to phrases like: "He wouldn't look
me in the eye," and "She is shifty-eyed." Study after study

has shown that children grow healthier physically and emotionally when their mothers gaze at them lovingly. With the benefits of eye-to-eye contact reaching both your spouse and your children, reviewing your own ability to maintain a direct gaze and giving attention to improving your eye contact can do wonders for the communication within your home.

But how should eye-to-eye contact be maintained, without staring? If there is a heated discussion, maintaining an uninterrupted gaze may appear to be an angry gesture. If your child is trying to discuss something embarrassing or awkward, your eye-to-eye contact may make it all the more difficult for your child to complete what she is trying to say. So care and thought should be given to when and where to maintain uninterrupted eye contact during a conversation.

This being said, eye-to-eye contact is not as easy as it sounds. Some rare individuals find it immensely easy to maintain proper eye contact, but for the rest of us, practice makes perfect. If you find that you have trouble maintaining eye contact, don't just consider it a character flaw. There are steps you can take to improve your eye-to-eye contact skills, and thus improve your ability to effectively communicate with your spouse, your children, and others outside your home.

When you are talking to a group, eye contact is often difficult. If you maintain eye contact with one individual, all the other people feel neglected and ignored. However, if you look over their heads at the back of the room, they will know that you are not looking at them. This old technique of speaking to groups has been proven ineffective in giving listeners a sense of connection with the speaker. Rather than looking at just one person or the wall at the back of the room, make genuine eye contact with one person, then change to make genuine eye contact with another person when you change sentences. With each new sentence, change eye contact. This would even come in handy with a gathering of friends, your children sitting around the dinner table or when sharing with a group of co-workers.

How are we to maintain a consistent gaze when speaking one on one to our spouse or child without seeming a bit intense? Assuring the listener that you still have something to contribute can be done without staring them down during a conversation. The key is to break your gaze about every five seconds. When you do break your gaze do not look down. Looking down gives one of two impressions. The listener will either think that you are ashamed or lying, or they will assume that you no longer care and want to disengage from the conversation. Neither of these thoughts is in your heart, so you will want your eyes to communicate your intentions correctly.

In order to communicate your continued interest and integrity, simply look up or to the side like you are thinking about what to say next. This is the eye movement you will want to attempt when breaking your gaze. If you look up or to the side, then your listener will know that you are either pondering what to say or trying to remember a piece of information. This is an easy way to avoid staring at the listener, but still assuring them of your interest.

What is an effective way to break your gaze while listening to your spouse without giving the air of indifference? Try implementing the "triangle" approach to eye contact. While your husband is talking about his day at work, stare at his left eye for about five seconds, then look at his right eye for another five seconds, and then finally watch his mouth for the last five seconds. When this is done, begin the whole "triangle" again. This way you remain engaged, but don't offend with an unbroken stare.

As much as we all hate them, arguments do happen. When arguing, eye contact becomes even more important. While you are speaking in an argument, hold your peaceful gaze. If your spouse attempts to look away, kindly try to regain their gaze. Conversely, no matter how mad you are, maintain constant eye contact while your spouse is sharing their grievances. Looking away during an argument will always lead to misunderstood motives and hurt feelings.

A person who holds eye contact will come across more confident, believable, and respectable. We all want to be respected and believed. Your ability to hold a gaze during times of conflict will go a long way toward winning the much sought after respect of your spouse. However, be very careful not to glare angrily at your spouse. Regardless of the kind words you speak, the "words" spoken by angry eyes will be the sentences your spouse remembers long after the argument has been resolved.

Another reason why eye-to-eye contact is important is because there are times when we want to attract our spouse. Our eyes can go a long way toward communicating our desires to be close to our husband or wife. Stare into their eyes. Don't merely look AT their eyes, but try to mentally dive into their pupils. You will notice that their pupils will dilate the longer you stare at them. This is a natural response to someone you love. Simply holding their gaze can increase the bond between you. If you want an even closer bond, imagine being intimate with your mate. This will increase adrenaline and dilate your pupils even more. As they see your pupils dilate, it will let them know that they are desired, loved, and valued, all because you stared at them!

The eyes reveal so much about a person. Remember to tell positive stories when you let your eyes do the "talking." Again, in the Song of Songs 4:9 (NIVR) says, *"You have ravished my heart, my treasure, my bride. I am overcome by one glance of your eyes, by a single bead of your necklace."* Your glance, even when you two may not be getting along, really does matter to your spouse. Your eyes can negotiate when your mouth can't. Try it!

Key #4

Think Before You Speak

"The heart of the godly thinks carefully before speaking; the mouth of the wicked overflows with evil words." (Proverbs 15:28 NLT)

Good communication is much more than the words spoken. In fact, communication is only as good as the thought that takes place prior to the words leaving your mouth. Little thought may result in poorly received communication. Careful thoughtfulness, on the other hand, leads to effective communication, which has the best chance for sending the intended message and making the intended impact on the recipient.

Have you ever been caught off guard by your own words? You know the scenario. You are in a discussion with someone and you just blurt out the first thing that comes to your mind and then immediately wish you could take it back. We've all been there. The problem with this type of communication is that it not only can make you look bad but it can also cause pain to others. Whether the blurted words are hurtful to the recipient or could be considered gossip that is hurtful to others, you want to avoid allowing words to leave your mouth without thinking first.

Small children are a great example of speaking without thinking. In fact, most four-year-olds speak and speak and speak the very first thoughts that come to mind, often to their parents' embarrassment. While this kind of talk can be excused for a four-year-old, there comes a time when it becomes unacceptable. Even older children must be taught to develop their communication by "filtering" what they say so they can learn when to hold their tongues and how to speak appropriately in certain situations.

Proverbs 18:13 (The Message) explains, *"Answering before listening is both stupid and rude."* Whoa! Sounds harsh, but it is so true. When you blurt out a response without thinking about the words, chances are you are also not truly listening to the other person's words or paying attention to his or her demeanor. Responding in this way opens the door to anger or confusion from the other person, which can in turn cause them to stop listening to you. This is clearly not the path to healthy or effective communication.

What does it mean to think before speaking? How does one do this without appearing slow or stupid? Of course, you don't want there to be minutes of silence as you formulate your response. This may seem a little too calculated and may even lead to distrust from the recipient. But, there is nothing wrong with taking a deep breath and a few seconds to think. It may even be helpful to state, "I want to accurately express myself, so I'm going to take a couple of seconds to get my words together." This statement is honest and makes the recipient know you care about the discussion.

Again, we can look to Proverbs to gain perspective on how we should respond with our words: *"Reckless words pierce like a sword, but the tongue of the wise brings healing"* (12:18). While we may have grown up hearing the common saying—sticks and stones may break my bones, but words will never hurt me—this is actually a very incorrect statement. There is great power in words. Reckless, thoughtless words can and do hurt others and even ourselves. Striving to have a "wise tongue" is the key to avoiding pain and miscommunication.

The wise communicator considers the recipient's position before speaking. They survey the person's stance, demeanor, and facial expressions. When the wise communicator senses defensiveness or anger, they know they must carefully select words to diffuse anger, words that empathize with the recipient, avoiding accusations at all cost. It is very difficult for the recipient to respond in anger at the communicator when they are showing compassion and empathy with their words. Finding a way to begin the conversation with kind words, allows the communicator to continue speaking about the issue once the recipient is no longer feeling defensive or hurt.

An example of this is a woman who needs to talk with her husband about helping more with the kids and the house. She is very frustrated with his lack of help and wants to find a way to effectively communicate her desire for assistance without offending him and causing strife in the marriage. She knows if she angers her husband with her words, he is much less likely to give her the help she wants and needs.

One night her husband mentions that he plans to play basketball with friends after work the following day. Initially, upon hearing the plans, the woman becomes angry and her first reaction is to snap at him and say something sarcastic. Instead, she takes a couple of seconds, pulls in her emotions, and tries to be a wise communicator.

"Honey, I would really like to talk with you more about stuff going on around the house. I'm feeling a little overwhelmed by everything and need your help to make things work as well as they possibly can. It's hard for me when you are gone so often. Is there any way we can work it out, so that I can have your help with the kids and the house?"

This communication is an example of a woman expressing herself; the situation details her feelings without accusing her husband or nagging him about his responsibilities. She could have easily told him that he wasn't being responsible and that he was expecting her to do everything. She could have said it wasn't fair and that she was tired of his lack of help. These things might even be true, yet it isn't always the best thing to state them out right. Instead, the wise woman considered her words and her husband's position. She realized he probably wasn't thinking and perhaps didn't even realize how much help she needed around the house – because she makes it look seamless.

Choosing her words carefully and speaking out of love, not anger, set up the discussion to have a positive tone. She was direct in that she asked her husband for his help, but she did not demand anything of him or belittle him with her words. It is never easy to communicate with someone once they are feeling defensive. A good communicator knows this and avoids offending someone at all costs. The reason is that the offended person will likely cease listening at that moment. Communication can no longer be effective or productive if one of the parties is offended. So it is particularly important to begin a conversation in a complimentary tone, speaking out of love and avoiding angry tones.

James tells us, *"Understand this, my dear brothers and sisters: You must all be quick to listen, slow to speak, and slow to get angry. Human anger does not produce the righteousness God desires"* (James 1:19-20 NLT). Reining in one's anger is key in healthy communication. Whether that looks like a taking a few moments to gather one's thoughts and emotions, or saying a quick prayer asking for God's help to eliminate angry thoughts, it is important to avoid lashing out in anger or speaking words without thinking first.

A couple drove down a country road for several miles, not saying a word. An earlier discussion had led to an argument and neither of them wanted to concede their position. As they passed a barnyard of mules, goats, and pigs, the husband asked sarcastically, "Relatives of yours?" "Yep," the wife replied, "in-laws."

Key #5

Praying Together, Staying Together

"Again I say to you, that if two of you agree on earth about anything that they may ask, it shall be done for them by My Father who is in heaven." (Matthew 18:19 NASB)

Prayer is fundamental in any relationship. It is your opportunity to communicate with your Creator. It can deepen the intimacy of your relationship with God and help you to obtain the strength and peace you need to make it through the day. Prayer can also be key in developing effective communication with others in your life. Whether it is your spouse, friend, parent or child, praying together facilitates agreement and unity and puts God in His proper place—at the center of your communication and relationships.

Ecclesiastes 4:12 explains that one person standing alone can be attacked and defeated, but two can come together and conquer. It states that *"three are even better, for a triple-braided cord is not easily broken."* The third person is unquestionably God. This analogy shows that praying includes God into your relationship and makes you stronger and able to conquer struggles that may come your way.

As you and your spouse pray, you strengthen your marriage exponentially. You are giving your relationship power—spiritual power that improves your lives as a couple as well as individuals.

Opposites attract. Is this true in your marriage? Whether it is 100% the truth or not, chances are you and your spouse differ in some areas. Even if you have similar temperaments or interests, there are probably certain issues that can cause a disagreement. It is okay! God created each of you as individuals. The beautiful thing is that with God even two of the most different individuals can come together in unity through prayer. God gives us the ability to do impossible things if we allow Him to help us.

I can recall early in my marriage I thought it was some sort of cruel joke that my new husband and I saw things from such different perspectives. I would read books hoping to find the key to understanding this man to whom I had pledged my love and life. Book after book would explain that most women and men were very different and would not naturally see things in the same way. Some authors would even go as far as to say it was as if men were from a different planet. At times, this theory wasn't too hard for me to believe, yet I wasn't satisfied with it. I wanted to understand my husband more and to have unity in our marriage. I just believed in my heart that is what God wanted, too. Books will give you general knowledge, wisdom, and some understanding based on male and female relationships or from the author's perspective but only God can give you insight on how YOU should communicate with YOUR spouse.

Once I began to realize that God created man and woman differently for a distinct purpose, it eased my anxiety and helped me to not only embrace our differences but also become thankful for them. As we trust that every experience and relationship we have in our lives has the potential to glorify God, it can provide a fresh perspective. It also provides a sense of adventure—trying to glorify God in even challenging and difficult circumstances. For me, once I learned that my husband and I had to have God in the center of our lives in order to have a healthy and fruitful relationship, it made all the difference. We knew that if we wanted our marriage to be successful, we had to strive to glorify Him and look to Him to bring us together in unity. One of the most important ways to glorify Him was to simply include Him through prayer.

As we spend time praying together and deepening our individual relationships with God, we naturally grow closer to one another because as we start to love God with all our hearts, minds and souls, He teaches us how to love others as. You've heard that marriage is reflective of Jesus' love for us. He is the husband and we (Christians) are the bride. The closer we (Christians, men and women) connect to Him and love Him, it rolls over into our marriages. When we understand and appreciate His love, forgiveness, and peace, we can extend it to our loved ones. His love connects us and brings us into unity with each other and with God. What a powerful display of God's impact on a marriage if we choose to let Him in!

As you can see, prayer with your spouse is key. The impact the prayer of a couple can make far exceeds the prayer of just one. Matthew 19 shows Jesus giving an important message about the prayer of more than one person: *"Again I say to you, that if two of you agree on earth about anything that they may ask, it shall be done for them by My Father who is in heaven. For where two or three have gathered together in My name, there I am in their midst"* (19-20). While it is important to pray with your spouse, it is more important to have an individual relationship with God and spend time in personal Bible study and prayer so He can teach you how to be successful in your relationship even though only one is praying.

While many marriages in the world around us split for causes such as "irreconcilable differences," we, as Christians, have the answer for a marriage challenged by differences: God. The problem is that even many married Christians don't go to God with their struggles. In fact, nearly a fourth of all Christian marriages end in divorce—this percentage is only slightly lower than non-Christian marriages.

To make a Christian marriage work, it takes more than simply taking on the label Christian. Without praying together, you might as well throw out the phrase "Christian marriage." A Family Life (www.familylife.org) study revealed that less than 8% of married couples that consider themselves Christians pray together. Less than 8%! How can couples experience God's healing power in the marriages without joining together in prayer?

If taking time out of each day to pray together seems like too much initially, consider making time once a week. Make an appointment, just like you would for any other meeting. Maybe even mark it on your calendars. During this meeting, join together in thanking God for your marriage and asking Him to guide each of you as you work to strengthen your union. You may be amazed by the power a simple prayer with your spouse can bring. Hearts can be softened. Walls can be torn down. Leave it to God to do something great in your marriage through your simple act of prayer.

Key #6

Write the Vision

"Write the vision and make it plain on tablets, that he may run who reads it. For the vision is yet for an appointed time; but at the end it will speak, and it will not lie. Though it tarries, wait for it; because it will surely come, it will not tarry" (Habakkuk 2:2-3)

Writing is another form of communicating. When Lewis and I were engaged, a pastor told us to sit down and write a vision for our family. It was a great exercise because it made us come into agreement about certain things. Although some things have not come to pass as of yet or goals have changed, we constantly review it and adjust it. The point is things change, we've changed, but the vision keeps us focused and gives us purpose as a couple.

Write a vision for your family. Even spouses who are polar opposites agreed on enough things to want to marry each other. Therefore, you should be able to effectively voice your goals and visions, your hopes and dreams. Not all of yours will match your spouse's, but not all of them have to. Perhaps, the only thing you can agree on is that you want to send your children to college. This future goal can often get overshadowed by the fact that you don't agree on how many children, if you're willing to adopt, or discipline of the children. However, sharing the same vision can go a long way in smoothing over the rough patches of disagreement. Granted, it is much easier to focus on what we don't have in common and on goals we don't share. But, if we can turn our focus on what we do have in common and agree on the goals, the divorce rate would decrease.

This agreement can become a solidifying factor in your daily walk together. 1 Corinthians 1:10 says, *"I appeal to you, brothers, in the name of our Lord Jesus Christ, that all of you agree with one another so that there may be no divisions among you and that you may be perfectly united in mind and thought."* This verse suggests that agreement does not come as a result of already being united in mind and thought. Instead, agreeing brings about unity of mind and thought. The more we agree, the more unified we will become. What a wonderful thing to have as a goal: a marriage with no divisions and unity of thought!

A few years ago, there was much buzz, even in the secular world, about author Rick Warren's book *Purpose Driven Life.* In it Warren used the Bible to show people how to discover their God-given purpose. There's something appealing about knowing your purpose in life. Without feeling like you have a purpose, life can become confusing and even feel pointless, to the point where you are continually searching and thinking there's more to life than being married to your spouse. Most marriages end in divorce because with no vision, they perish (Proverbs 29:18). As Christians, we can trust that God has a purpose for our lives and our marriage. He created each spouse and has an individual vision for each, as well as a vision for the couple; it can be a purpose-driven union if we allow God to plant dreams in our hearts for our marriages.

Yes, we can enjoy God's blessings here on earth, but our purpose is not to please ourselves, regardless of the self-serving messages we receive from the rest of the world. So once we get the fact that we are here for God's pleasure to serve Him, love Him and love His people as He commanded, it gives our lives new meaning. In the same way, it absolutely gives our marriages new meaning as well.

Our individual mission: to love God, love others, and tell others about God. Our marital mission: to love God, love others, and tell others about God. Yep, it's the same. The difference is that in marriage you have the benefit of working together as a team. Allowing God to plant a dream for your marriage in your heart means that you are allowing God to use your team for His purposes and glory. It makes your marriage so much more than a ceremony, some paperwork and having babies (not that children aren't a blessing!).

Perhaps God has given you a vision to open your home to people in need by providing meals and hospitality. Or maybe He has given you and your spouse gifts to share with others, such as singing, preaching, or serving on the mission field. Other possible dreams from God might be starting a Christ-centered business or non-profit organization or leading a Bible study in your neighborhood.

There is no limit to God, so the possibilities for what God can do through your marriage are limitless. Once you have given God the green light and made yourself and your marriage available for His purposes, you can be certain He will make things happen.

So how do you give God the "green light" and discover what your dream and purpose are for your marriage?

Check out these key points:

- **Pray**—Prayer is an important place to start. Make a point to pray together, asking God to strengthen your relationship and place a dream in each of your hearts. As discussed in Chapter 5, prayer brings unity and agreement—both of these are of utmost importance when you are striving for a purposeful marriage.

- **Get wisdom**—It's hard to hear from God when you aren't studying His word. God speaks through the Bible—the Word is inspired and powerful and can direct your steps. It is a lamp to your feet and a light to your path (Psalm 119:105). This means you and your spouse can know where you should be going and what you should be doing when you seek God through the Bible. Whether you do it individually or together, do it, and share with each other what you learn.

- **Practice trust and selfless love**—God definitely has a vision and a purpose for your life—these plans are to prosper you and not to hurt you; they are to give you a hope and a future (Jeremiah 29:11). You can put your trust in His dream for your life and marriage. However, to truly place your trust in God, you must learn to live and love selflessly. When you can truly be okay with bringing glory to God, rather than glory to yourself, God is going to give you a dream.

- **Dream together**—Don't be afraid to share your hopes and dreams with your spouse. If you have been praying, getting wisdom from the Word, and putting your trust in God, you can feel confident about sharing your heart with you spouse. Consider writing down short-term and long-term visions for your marriage. If you each take some time to do this individually and then come together to compare notes, it is fun to recognize the similarities and then to stretch each other with new ideas.

Lack of dreams in your marriage can cause things to go stale quickly. Making the effort to dream breathes new life into a marriage relationship. It's like finding inspiration for your life together. When struggles and challenges come, a dream or vision can help you to make it through and keep you focused on the goal. Also, dreams create a sense of fulfillment. Your marriage becomes much more than the day-to-day events and responsibilities, because you have a God-given purpose that guides you and stretches you.

While it may be tempting from time to time focus on individual goals, sometimes this can cause disunity in a marriage. The spouse who becomes overly focused on individual dreams can inadvertently alienate his partner. For example, a man who chooses to go after his career dream may have to put the best part of his time and energy into the dream. While he is busy improving his skills and setting goals, his wife is battling loneliness and frustration. Because God created marriage to fulfill a unified purpose and dream, when one spouse goes his own way negative consequences can result for the marriage. When you include your spouse and God in on your goal-setting and dreams, you can know you have the power of the Lord on your side. It can be a beautiful time of increased intimacy and unity when you work toward a goal as a team with your partner and God.

Key #7

Know Your Spouse

"Bear one another's burdens, and thereby fulfill the law of Christ." (Galatians 6:2 NASB)

While premarital counseling is becoming more and more popular within Christian and secular circles alike, there are still many couples who walk down the aisle without receiving formal counsel. One of the primary benefits to counseling during an engagement is that the future bride and groom have an opportunity to discuss their individual backgrounds and experiences and discover how these will affect their relationship in the future. Marriage is a new journey, but it is inevitable that the past—whether it be negative experiences, former relationships, or family issues—will shape the relationship, particularly communication between husband and wife.

If you missed out on premarital counseling or didn't exactly deal with real issues prior to your wedding, it isn't too late to benefit your marriage and communication through an examination of the past. It is important to first recognize the significant impact the past can have on your relationship. Avoid minimizing or dismissing painful experiences in your spouse's history. Doing so prevents further wounding and helps your spouse to feel more comfortable sharing issues from their past. A spouse who takes on the perspective that "the past is the past," may not only cause the partner to go into a shell but may also stop marital growth and communication.

Identifying and discussing the factors from the past that affect your relationship can help you to turn even negative experiences and influences into relationship strengths. There is no reason that a woman or man who was reared in an unstable family environment can't experience a healthy marriage relationship. However, these past issues cannot be swept under the rug. Dealing with them through formal counseling, open communication, or both paves the way to a strong marriage.

There is no doubt about it—our past life experiences shape who we are today. An individual who grew up in a poor home may have a fear of going without necessities. Such a fear may present itself as behaviors ranging from pinching pennies, to overspending, to hoarding. Instead of seeing these behaviors as a character flaws, this person's spouse should take the time to understand the reasons behind the behavior.

You may be surprised how connected your spouse's behaviors are to hurtful issues from their past. Many husbands and wives think they know their spouses well when, in fact, there are huge parts of their history they know nothing about. For many people, they simply don't feel close enough to their spouses or safe enough to share the details of their past. For others, the level of conversation stays at, "What's for dinner?" or "Did you pay the electric bill?"

We know God created marriage so two people could come together, help each other, and honor Him with their union.

Genesis 2:25 tells us *"And the man and his wife were both naked and were not embarrassed or ashamed in each other's presence."* For this reason, we need to get the issues out in the open in order to work through them and heal. Discussing past hurts and issues should lead to deeper intimacy within the marriage. However, this mean's moving past one's comfort zone and going deeper than, "What's for dinner?" It also means that as we heal we will be even more ready to make our marriage what God intended it to be, and we will be blessed for our efforts to strengthen our marriages, which is honoring to God.

What does it mean to discuss the issues with your spouse? In the example of the spouse raised in poverty, you can talk about how his or her experience with poverty creates a sense of fear. You can help the spouse to verbalize what you can do to help ease fears in a healthy way. Opening up a discussion about such issues in a compassionate and loving way can only improve communication and increase intimacy between husband and wife. Also, when an argument over money erupts, you will understand that the root of it is based on fear and you can address it from that standpoint versus a defensive position.

Issues that significantly affect marriages include parental attachment, divorce, finances, dating relationships, friendships, physical appearance, religion, discipline, military background, education, racism, medical, molestation, and many more. What may seem to be a small issue to one person may be a deep wound to another, so it is important to discuss issues from the past with sensitivity.

Entering into counseling with a professional Christian counselor may be ideal for couples facing serious issues from the past. However, for people with less intense issues, it is possible to create your own little counseling sessions at home, as long as you can provide for each other an environment that is safe and loving.

Taking the time to truly examine issues from the past can go a long way in strengthening your marriage and communication, but it takes some work. It does not come naturally for all people to have empathy for each other and listen carefully to details of the past. In fact, it may be a real stretch for some spouses to take on a counselor-like role. However, we, as Christians, have been called to be more and more like Jesus who was known as Wonderful Counselor (Isaiah 9:6). He was known for being loving and compassionate—the perfect model for a spouse. As we keep this in mind, it becomes easier to offer our ears and heart to our husband or wife.

You may be at a loss as how to take on the counselor-like role for your spouse. You may not even know where to begin when it comes to deeper issues of the past. Here are a few ideas to get you started, as you learn more about each other's histories and how they affect your relationship today:

- Find a quiet time without distractions to start the discussion. A date night in a private spot in a restaurant or a night at home after the kids are in bed are possibilities. The key is to prevent distractions. There should be no television on in the background. Turn the ringer off on your phones.

- Give your full attention to you spouse. Ask open-ended questions, but don't get angry or offended if your spouse isn't eager to answer all your questions. He or she may not yet be ready to share all things. The fact that you have made the effort and opened the door to communication is an important first step.

- Be willing to listen without offering advice. Often, husbands are known for trying to "fix" their wives problems. Some wives complain that they can't share struggles and frustrations with their husbands, because they won't just listen to them, they have to offer solutions. Whether you are the husband or the wife, do your best to listen without trying to solve problems or correct your spouse. No one who is sharing sensitive information from the past wants to hear, "Well, you should have done...." A good counselor is an excellent listener.

- Offer unconditional love and affection. Remind your spouse that you love him no matter what has happened in his past. If she becomes emotional, offer your hand to hold or ask if you can hug her. These acts of kindness will help him or her to feel comfortable and loved.

- Ask your spouse what you can do to help them to heal from past wounds. Let them know you want to help them through it.

- Discuss together how some of the issues you face today in your marriage may be related to your past experiences. Perhaps there are generational patterns you see in your lives that you want to work together to change. Make a list of issues, pray about them, and meet together regularly to discuss how you are doing.

God's idea for marriage is much more than a partnership, parenthood, or even companionship. He designed husband and wife to help each other through life—to be Jesus to one another, ultimately bringing glory to God. Taking the time and effort to work through issues, past and present, is of utmost importance as you strive to reach toward your own 'happily ever after' relationship.

Key #8

Spouses Are Not Mind Readers

*"…Then all the churches will know that I am He who
searches hearts and minds, and I will repay each of you
according to your deeds." (Revelation 2:23 NIV)*

Wouldn't it be great to be married to a mind reader? Yes, it sounds silly, but so many husbands and wives have this expectation for their spouses. They don't want to tell them what they want; they just want them to know. In other words, they want them to be mind readers! From birthday presents to words of endearment to more intimate issues, spouses all over the world somehow expect their beloved to know exact what they desire. This is a pretty lofty expectation, and it almost always leads to failure and disappointment. Learning to communicate your wishes and desires effectively and with love is one of the keys to good marital communication.

"If he loved me, he would know." We've all heard these words from a friend or maybe they've come out of our own mouths. Unfortunately, many spouses have this attitude. They tell themselves that if their spouse truly loved them, he or she would innately know the right things to say and do. Simply put, this is a lie. God gave us language in order to communicate with each other and express ourselves, but He didn't gift us with mind reading capabilities—although some may disagree.

Think of it this way: Does God expect us to guess what is right and wrong or does He lay it out for us? That's easy, right? God has provided His Holy Word (Bible) and the Holy Spirit, so we can know all about Him, His likes and dislikes, so that we can know how to grow closer and closer to Him. He has given us directions to obtaining a relationship with Him (Romans 10:9), as well as how to strengthen it (John 15:7). In the same way, we must lovingly verbalize our likes and dislikes, hopes and desires, to our spouses. God doesn't make us guess when it comes to knowing how to show Him love (see John 14:15), just like we should not have to guess what our spouse desires.

So, go ahead and throw "if he/she loved me" out the window. God—who is LOVE—provided direction, therefore, so can we. For some people, expressing wants and desires is downright difficult. Individuals who have people-pleaser characteristics especially struggle with being assertive when it comes to personal needs and preferences. People pleasers may need more encouragement from spouses in order to share expectations. Because they have trained themselves to focus on others' pleasure, they may feel out of element verbalizing what they want.

A people-pleasing wife once shared her story about learning to express her desires. As a young working mother of three children under age four, she struggled to accomplish her goals each day. She resented her husband because it seemed like he was taking it easy after work and enjoying life, while she was scrambling around cooking, cleaning and caring for children. Occasionally, her husband would ask if he could do something, but she would quickly say no, as she didn't want him to become annoyed or think she couldn't handle things.

Finally, one evening during a particularly busy and stressful week, she had an emotional breakdown. When she calmed down enough to talk with her husband, she shared with him that she resented his seemingly carefree evenings, while she worked so hard. He said to her, "I can't remember one, single time you have asked me to do anything for you." It was then that she realized he was right. She had not expressed her struggles or need for his help. Even when he offered, she dismissed him.

After this night, husband and wife began working as a team. Her husband had to remind her to ask for help, but little by little she began to overcome her people-pleasing tendencies, learning to express her desires. This story is quite similar to the woman who says she doesn't want a Valentine's gift, yet is depressed when she doesn't receive anything. It is completely unfair to one's spouse to expect something without allowing him to know what it is, and it is even worse when you say one thing and expect another. That is called playing mind games, and it has no place in a loving, honest Christian marriage.

It may take practice to learn to speak one's mind, but it is worth the effort. Good communication in marriage is about being transparent and authentic. If this level of honesty in communication is new to your marriage, consider making a formal effort to incorporate it into your life together. One way to do this might be to set aside time each day (or weekly) to have a "sharing time." During this time each spouse will share one thing the other has done that has been a blessing, and then one desire or want he/she has. The beauty of this activity is that you are complimenting each other and finding a way to express your needs in an open format.

While it may be overwhelming for someone to express desires during day-to-day activities, setting aside a special "sharing time" helps to take some of the fear out of the process. Since both spouses are sharing together, the hesitant spouse may be more comfortable voicing her desires. What is especially helpful about such an activity is that within a few weeks, both parties will become more at ease when it comes to giving compliments, accepting compliments, and expressing desires. Chances are, in time there will be little need for a specific "sharing time," because it will become a normal part of your lives.

If communication is a struggle for husband and wife, it is of utmost importance to make an effort to improve it. When one or both people suppress desires, bitterness develops and builds a wall between spouses. As more time passes, bitterness can turn into indifference, which is obviously not the goal for any relationship—particularly a God-honoring marriage.

As more and more marriages seem to be under attack, it seems Satan is making his move, building walls and turning spouses against each other. Choose to fight for your marriage by placing a high importance on communication with your spouse, and know God is on your side. He wants what is best for you and your spouse, and He wants to see your marriage succeed. When you are at the end of your rope and feel you are tired of making the effort, cling to God and pray for His help. He is the master of all things good—communication, love and marriage—and He will help you through the hard times if you allow Him. And He is the only mind reader!

A man and his wife were having an argument about who should brew the coffee each morning. The wife said, "You should do it because you get up first, and then we don't have to wait as long to get our coffee. The husband said, "You are in charge of cooking around here and you should do it, because that is your job, and I can just wait for my coffee." Wife replies, "No, you should do it, and besides, it is in the Bible that the man should do the coffee." Husband replies, "I can't believe that, show me." So she fetched the Bible, and opened the New Testament and showed him at the top of several pages, that it indeed says .... "HEBREWS".

Key #9

Meeting Great Expectations

> *"My soul, wait thou only upon God; for my
> expectation is from him."* (Psalms 62:5)

Many relationship experts agree on one thing that often leads to trouble in marriages: unmet expectations. It usually begins before the wedding even takes place. The bride-to-be dreams of endless romance and special times together, while the expectant groom dreams of lots of time in the bedroom. Okay—so that may be a bit stereotypical, so let's try another possible scenario: The bride envisions taking lavish vacations together with her new husband, while the groom looks forward to saving and investing to prepare for their future and retirement years.

Regardless of the situation, expectations for the marriage begin before the bride and groom say "I do." Perhaps the best way to deal with expectations prior and during marriage is to keep the lines of communication open—and deal with reality together. While there is no need to think you must have low expectations for your spouse (or worse yet, no expectation), there is such a thing as healthy expectations expressed to your spouse in a loving way.

Truly healthy marriages are comprised of selfless individuals who put the other person's needs before their own. This person isn't a doormat, but rather a God follower who knows that he or she has been called to show true love to others—love that is kind, protects, hopes, perseveres and is not self-seeking (1 Cor. 13). When each spouse is showing this kind of love to each other, the focus will naturally be on meeting the other person's expectations. He or she will not be focusing on personal desires but rather on those of the spouse's.

For example, a wife who appreciates structure and schedules likes to know when her husband will be home for dinner. Because the couple wants to try to have the evening meal together each night, she strives to time the meal just right, so it will be hot and ready when her husband walks through the door. If her husband is going to be late, he calls her to let her know as soon as he knows, because he realizes how important it is to his wife to know when he is on is way. He is meeting a reasonable expectation his wife has to know when he will be home or if he plans to be late. Although it may inconvenience him slightly to stop what he is doing and pick up the phone to inform her, he makes the effort because he honors her expectation and is putting her needs before his own.

Likewise, the wife does not become enraged if her husband gets tied up and forgets to phone her. She puts herself in his shoes, realizing the stress of his job, knowing that he usually remembers to call her and next time he probably will. She is taking the focus off of herself and her frustration of wanting to have a hot meal together at a certain time and putting the focus on her husband and showing him love by being forgiving and kind.

What is special about this couple is that each spouse is striving to put the other first. Selfishness—one of the most common culprits of failing marriages—is out the window. While neither spouse is perfect, each is making an effort to show selfless love; therefore, there is peace and respect between them. Because oneness is incompatible with selfishness, it is impossible to find true unity in marriage when selfishness reigns in both partners. Our human nature is sinful, therefore, it feels natural to be self-focused, but with God we can learn to change our ways to become more like Him, seeing the other person as He sees them. When we do this, we find that our expectations are fulfilled, as we are simultaneously better meeting the expectations of our spouse.

While it is no easy task to become selfless, it is possible with God's help. For people who have been hurt in the past, it can be especially difficult to surrender the self-focus. Wounded people often develop defense mechanisms to protect themselves from further pain. A common defense mechanism is to demand a certain level of treatment from others. If the demands and expectations are unmet, the wounded person may retaliate by lashing out or not communicating at all with the other person or fleeing the relationship. They do this in order to avoid being hurt again. They feel like if they keep a sense of control in the situation—control being their expectation—they can control the other person's behavior, thus, protecting themselves. However, when we allow God to heal our wounds, we are better able to give up control and release certain expectations. It is only then, that the wounded person can achieve true oneness in a marriage relationship.

It can be challenging, but it is worth the effort to do our best to put our spouse first. The marital rewards are rich: true companionship, peace in the marriage, relational fulfillment. Two self-less people joined in marriage can experience the kind of relationship the way God intended it to be. It also helps us to become more like Christ, strengthening and enriching our relationship with God. Once we have experienced this unique closeness with our spouse, times of separation and divorce are far less likely. In the same way, we are less likely to stray from God once we have truly experienced a real relationship with Him.

Praying and learning much about the characteristics of God through the Bible are great ways to prepare yourself for selflessness and true love. Consider asking your spouse to pray with you and make commitments to God and each other to rid selfishness from your marriage. Ask your spouse to list some ways you can bless him by meeting certain expectations he has for the marriage. Hopefully, they will ask you the same. If not, you know that you are working with a selfish person.

There may be times in your marriage in which one spouse is more self-focused than others. During these times, it is best for the other spouse to simply cling to God and keep on serving God and the spouse. Love is much more likely to win over the struggling spouse than anger or acts of retaliation. James 3:16 tells us that selfishness leads to confusion (disharmony) and all sorts of evil practices); therefore, one person needs to bring harmony into the marriage by demonstrating selflessness. By continuing to honor the spouse by meeting expectations and showing love, you will essentially be honoring God with your life and your marriage.

Key #10

Understanding Communication Styles

*"Teach me, and I will be quiet; show me where
I have been wrong." (Job 6:24 NIV)*

Good communication involves more than simply staying
quiet while your spouse is talking. Our own perceptions,
for good or for bad, filter the verbal information we hear.
We, as humans, can wrongly assign motives, misunderstand
what is said, or underestimate another person's attempt to
communicate. We must safeguard ourselves against these
traps if we truly want a rich and rewarding marriage and
healthy communication with our spouse.

We are the result of our pasts. Our upbringing, our
tragedies, our successes, our losses, and our gains all work
together to effect both how we see the world and how we
interact with it. Attempting to understand the intricate
past that wove the fabric of your wife or husband will go
a long way toward seeing the beauty in their design. It can
also pinpoint potential snags, and with enough warning
you can correct them before they occur.

No doubt you both found out about each other's pasts
during your courtship. However, pieces of the puzzle will
continue to surface throughout the life of your marriage.
This is by no means to insinuate that your spouse withheld

the information, but that we each are complex individuals whose stories aren't done but are consistently being written. Simply knowing the events of their past like a record of facts is not enough to bring about healthy communication.

Consider your spouse, but not just like the man whose underwear you launder. Study them like you would study a character from a movie or a book. What makes him tick? What are her main motivations in light of her past experiences?

As an exercise, write down five major events in your spouse's past, good or bad. Study them and try to pinpoint some of the assumptions, desires, or philosophies your spouse may have derived from having gone through these events. This will be a powerful step toward understanding your mate. More than likely, the conclusions he or she draws from these past experiences will affect the way she or he responds in new situations.

In this way, knowing your spouse will explain the feelings behind what he says or does not say. Most of the breakdown in communication does not happen when we stop talking. The major communication crises take place when we are still talking, but no longer understanding what the other is saying. To deter this deaf ear, as it were, try to always consider your spouse. Even the way they word their sentences can be a result of their upbringing. Take that into consideration before assuming the worst. Notice their body language and eye contact. If you do not detect anger or frustration in their body language, do not jump to the conclusion that their words are hostile. And if you do detect anger, consider they may just be loud or passionate about the topic.

Furthermore, create the same list of five most influential events in your own life (i.e. divorced parents, an abusive parent). Look at yourself as if you were another person. Your past experiences definitely change your perception of the present. Knowing what your "triggers" are can help you discern whether you are reacting to the current discussion with your spouse or whether you are really filtering the current experience through a lens you fashioned years ago. Correctly understanding ourselves paves the way to correctly understanding those around us.

Now that the past is sufficiently studied, try to pinpoint what effect it has had on the communication style of you and your spouse. For example, was your wife physically abuse or intimidated? She may be indirect with her communication as a result. This stems from a fear of the truth leading to abuse. Was your husband lied to by a former girlfriend? This may result in repeatedly asking the same question to make sure you have the same answer each time. Knowing their background doesn't just help us understand their reasoning, but also gives us insights into how better to be understood.

Continuing on with the previous examples, we will take a look at how practical application can be made of the past experiences of our spouses. For the husband of a formerly abused wife, he can better understand her hesitancy to speak forthrightly. He no longer has to feel deceived. This may mean he has to coax a real opinion from her. This should be done in quiet, affirming tones. To be better heard and understood, he may want to try sitting so his physical height does not become a barrier to her listening to the true intent of his heart.

If her husband has been lied to, a wife should be patient with his distrust rather than frustrated. If she has nothing to hide, why not let him look through her purse or listen to her voice mail? If this sort of behavior goes on for a period of time, yes counseling needs to be sought. It does the husband no good to allow his paranoia to continue and increase. But in the early stages of courtship and marriage, his lack of trust should be addressed with kindness and patience. She may have to go a little out of her way to show him that he can trust her. Should you have to? No, but you do it because you love him and because he can trust you.

Your spouse's past may also contribute to the type of communication they find easiest. Perhaps living in a family with six children has led your spouse to speak loudly. Or maybe, being ignored has silenced your wife. Growing up with a lack of physical affection may prompt your husband to use touch to communicate favor. If a spouse grew up in abject poverty, generosity may be the number one way they choose to communicate love to you and your children.

Knowing how your spouse communicates is only the beginning of the listening process. You must be able to receive this communication and appreciate it for what it is, a loving gesture. If your spouse speaks loudly, you must remind yourself that he or she is not yelling. Receive the loud "I love you," as heartily as the soft one. Silence in a quiet spouse may mean she is at peace around you. Do not assume she is fuming mad just because she is quiet at any given moment. Resist the urge to cheapen a spouse's physical touch to mere lust. Many times, touch is an effective and compassionate way to communicate. Do not look at a gift given as "buying someone's affections," when really it is an act of love. (NOTE: I highly recommend the book, The Five Love Languages by Gary Chapman to help you in this area.)

Knowing your mate's love language should lead to respecting their way of "communicating" and allowing you to respond to them in that manner. If your husband uses physical touch to display affection, rather than telling him that you love him, walk over and rub his back. With this simple gesture, you are both affirming his style of communication and trying to speak his language. When a generous spouse gives you a gift following an argument, return the favor with an act of kindness or another gift. After receiving the gift say, "I love you, too." This acknowledges that you heard all that they were trying to say with the present.

As we grow in our knowledge and respect for our spouse, the more we should put our own agendas on the back burner. Love always wants more for the other than for itself. In studying our spouse's past and current communication style, we should listen to discern what they want rather than focus our attention on our desires. In understanding your mate's intricacies and communication styles you can alleviate those pesky arguments over what you THOUGHT they said, versus what they REALLY said. To hear, truly hear and to be heard, isn't that what we all want?

Key #11

Forgiving Each Other

"And become useful and helpful and kind to one another, tenderhearted (compassionate, understanding, loving-hearted), forgiving one another (readily and freely), as God in Christ forgave you." (Ephesians 4:32 AMP)

A life without forgiveness will lead to bitterness. It is so easy to allow bitterness to creep into our lives, especially when we have been deeply hurt by a spouse. However, it is impossible to have just a little bitterness. It grows and grows.

I will not let this bitter root grow in me.
I will not let you leave that legacy,
But it gets so hard when pain is all I see…

--Sara Groves, songwriter (Tornado)

As the song lyric above illustrates, it grows like a root, spreading its fingers throughout your life. Lack of forgiveness destroys marriages and lives all the time. We must strive to forgive others, even when we think they don't deserve it.

Pain in marriage is inevitable. Why? Because only those closest to you can hurt you. No matter how great of a spouse you are, you are still human. So is your husband or wife. Humans forget anniversaries, make thoughtless comments, lash out in anger, forget to call home, and the list goes on and on. Forgiveness is a calling we have as

Christians and a path to experience the life God wants for us. "Make allowance for each other's faults, and forgive anyone who offends you. Remember, the Lord forgave you, so you must forgive others" (Colossians 3:13). If we choose to hold onto the pain and keep the hurtful acts in our minds, we are practicing unforgiveness. The dangerous thing about unforgiveness is that it doesn't just make the person who made the mistake (intentional or unintentional) feel bad, it builds a wall between a husband and wife, and can destroy the life of the person who is unwilling to forgive.

Matthew 6:14-15 states, *"For if you forgive men when they sin against you, your heavenly Father will also forgive you. But if you do not forgive men their sins, your Father will not forgive your sins."* This in itself makes the perfect case for forgiveness. When we don't forgive our spouses, we cannot receive forgiveness for our sins. Anyone not need forgiveness? Of course not! We all need forgiveness. We are human and we are sinners, therefore, we must put ourselves in our offenders' shoes. Once we step back and see them as human, as sinners whom God loves and is willing to forgive, we may find ourselves more willing to extend forgiveness as well.

Also, if you simply start to feel annoyed with your spouse and are experiencing feelings of resentment, you need to check yourself to find out if there may be some lingering unforgiveness and bitterness. There was a time when Lewis was holding unforgiveness in his heart for years and I didn't know it. His attitude towards me had changed and I had no idea what I had done. Once we discussed it in counseling, we both realized that it was just a misunderstanding. For years he harbored these feelings which contributed to our marriage falling apart. It is so important to talk with your spouse about what they've done that hurt you. It probably is just a misunderstanding but at least if you discuss it, you can then start to deal with it.

There are times when we may not even realize we are struggling with unforgiveness. Each time we go to God praying for him to forgive our sins, we need to ask, "Is there anyone I need to forgive?" God will reveal it to you if you are holding on to something your spouse has done.

Ask God to search your heart, reveal the unforgiveness and help you to change your heart. Even when you feel like you don't want to forgive, you can ask God to change your heart. He can give you a true desire to forgive.

What if you feel like you deserve an apology, but there isn't one coming from your spouse? Take it to God. Again, you will not be forgiven for your sins if you do not forgive. The verse doesn't read, "...unless he/she doesn't offer you an apology." Nope. It simply commands you to forgive. Still, it can be difficult to forgive an unrepentant spouse. In the Bible, Peter tells us *"not to repay evil with evil or insult with insult, but with blessing, because to this you were called so that you may inherit a blessing"* (1 Peter 3:9). If you call upon the Lord to help you forgive, even in the case of an unrepentant spouse, you will be blessed.

Forgiveness is the number one step in repairing a broken relationship. Without it, the relationship will very likely fail. Whether the offense is small or very significant, God has called us to forgive just the same. He knows what is best for our lives and our marriages. Forgiving others provides freedom—not just for the offender, but also for the offended.

God gave the perfect example of forgiveness, when Jesus encountered the adulterous woman as reported in the Bible in John, Chapter 8. The woman had been caught in the act of adultery and dragged before Jesus by the angry Pharisees. They were ready to stone her. Jesus simply stated, *"If any of you are without sin, let him cast the first stone."*

Can you imagine being there in that moment? Jesus is saying the same thing to us when are ready to stone our spouse for his or her mistake. It may not be a literal stoning we have in mind—more like yelling, silent treatments, withholding affection, guilting. These "stones" can be just as painful to a spouse. And while it may feel good in the moment to blow off some steam, forgiveness is going to provide much more healing for you than any amount of stone throwing.

Forgiveness is not excusing misdeeds or saying it is okay to sin; it is about forgiving and loving despite your spouse's sin—just like Jesus does for us. It's called "turning the other cheek." It is important to recognize that every married couple experiences differences, because no two people are the same or perfectly compatible in every way. However, showing your spouse the grace that God shows you helps you to work through differences and challenges. It is a high calling and something we must practice in order to reach the level of His love being seen through our lives (read Matthew 5:38-42).

Perhaps once we learn that the sole purpose of marriage isn't just for personal enjoyment, it becomes easier to forgive. God created marriage to give humans companionship but most importantly He created it to bring glory to Himself. When we view our marriage as a journey—a path to bringing us closer to each other and to God—it makes sense to forgive each other and grow together.

Check your heart? Are you allowing unforgiveness to build a wall between you and your spouse? Whether the offensive episode was yesterday or ten years ago, it is time to extend forgiveness and free yourself from bitterness. When you forgive, you allow your relationship to be restored. Together you can rebuild it and strengthen it with God's blessing because you have obeyed His command to forgive and turn from sin. He calls us to forgive so that we can achieve the fulfilling marriage He desires for us.

Key #12

Recognizing the Power of Words

"Words kill, words give life; they're either poison or fruit—you choose." (Proverbs 18:21 MSG)

With all the discussion about body language and other nonverbal forms of communication, it is still wise to remember that words have power. What we say can and does affect the person to whom we are speaking, not to mention any others standing nearby. In the time we're living we are overrun by choices. We now have more choices in cappuccino flavors at a coffee shop than most western settlers had in grocery items at the town mercantile. We can choose to give life with our words. It is within our power to do so. With so many negative choices of words, why not opt to be kind? The phrase, "The pen is mightier than the sword," wasn't coined by a pretentious poet. It was made from mere observation. Words mean something.

Often, the negative words that go unsaid can greatly benefit the atmosphere of our homes. If you live with another human for more than a week, chances are at least one of you is going to get annoyed, frustrated, or even angry. The old adage that advises counting to ten before you speak is still sound advice. When a negative or criticizing thought enters your mind, first ask yourself if the words being considered will resolve or retaliate? Retaliation will get you nothing but more frustration.

If another person has unwittingly wounded you, yes you should speak up. However, if the way your husband goes on and on and on about basketball statistics is just pounding on your last nerve, stop before you tell him just where to go to watch the playoffs. If you can remove yourself from the situation, even to use the restroom, long enough to evaluate your words the negative words withheld will honor your spouse even while you are silent.

Many times these negative words or criticizing remarks are merely symptoms of an underlying lack of value for the other person. There are a few ways to see your spouse in a more valuable light. First, pray that God shows you His perspective on your spouse. As we know, God's affection for us is unfathomable. He adores your spouse, even when they are insensitive, cold, indifferent, or nagging. Rather than ask God to change your spouse, ask Him to change your perception of them or help you to change.

Secondly, resist the urge to compare your spouse to other people's spouses. During the times you two are not getting along, your spouse will never stand up to your scrutiny while you are consistently comparing his weaknesses to other people's strengths. Together, both of these approaches will help you value your spouse. Valuing the other person as a child of God will go a long way to keeping negative words at bay.

Another way is to complement them often so that you consistently see the good in them. Sincere complements, not just empty flattery, can also boost the self esteem of your spouse and keep compromised lines of communication open. There are times your husband can do no wrong in your estimation. Complements in those moments are too numerous to imagine. However, what happens in the rocky, arid times of our relationships? Even when you are resisting the temptation to compare and criticize, complements may not come easily. Determine to always be honest with your complements. If your husband is on the second straight hour of discussing basketball stats and players, complementing him with, "I just LOVE your enthusiasm about basketball," will not be believable.

It will sometimes be an all out scavenger hunt to find something positive about your spouse that you can HONESTLY praise her on, but the hunt is worth it. Even if your wife is a negative nag, she could still be a great housekeeper. If your husband is a lethargic, couch potato, he could tell the best jokes you've ever heard. In these types of situations, the husband can sincerely complement his wife on a beautiful home. Instead of complaining that her husband never does anything around the house, the wife could refrain from negative comments and honestly tell him how much she enjoys his jokes. Write a list of things you admire about your mate so you will be able to pull it out when you need to find a complement.

Finding genuine reasons to praise your spouse can avoid the pain of empty flattery. If you complement your spouse in a disingenuous way, it will have the opposite effect than what you desire. Choosing to complement them on something of no value (I love your shade of toe nail polish) or in a way that is obviously insincere (I love how you don't feel the need to shower like the other men) is deception. No matter how angry you are at your spouse, don't lie.

In addition, don't assume your affections are understood. Always tell your spouse that you love them. Reaffirming your love daily can have profoundly positive effects on your spouse. No matter how well you know your husband; his day at work, the traffic congestion on the way home and a horrible headache may have him a bit short tempered and distant. Assuring him that your love is a constant positive piece in his life may encourage him and empower your husband to face the challenges of the evening and days to follow.

Withholding negative criticism, verbalizing sincere compliments, and affirming your love have multiple positive benefits to the home environment. First and foremost, your spouse will feel valuable. Valuing someone will often lead to being heard by them. We, as humans, are more likely to respect someone's opinion when we perceive that they also respect us. Though, we must not try to negotiate someone else's behavior by using kind words. Your spouse may not return your positive words and affirmations. Don't be deterred. You are not choosing positive words in order to receive positive words in return. You are being nice, because it is the right thing to do. Kindness is always the correct response.

After all, it is God's kindness that leads us to repentance, not His nagging (Romans 2:4). Extending kindness to your spouse may have them wanting to change their behavior because they see God's kindness working through you. Continual negative speech will only weaken their resolve to change.

More importantly, if there are children in the home, viewing the mutual respect and honor between their parents will give them a sense of peace in their surroundings. It will encourage the same behavior in them. Children are more likely to honor their parents, when they witness their parents honoring one another on a daily basis. Moreover, they will carry these lessons of restraining negative comments, genuinely encouraging others and openly sharing their love into their schools, work places and eventually their marriages. If you train your children now, by example, on how to have a loving respectful home, they will reap a wonderful family of their own.

A man and his wife were having some problems at home and were giving each other the silent treatment. Suddenly, the man realized that the next day, he would need his wife to wake him at 5:00 AM for an early morning business flight. Not wanting to be the first to break the silence (and LOSE), he wrote on a piece of paper, "Please wake me at 5:00 AM." He left it where he knew she would find it. The next morning, the man woke up, only to discover it was 9:00 AM and he had missed his flight. Furious, he was about to go and see why his wife hadn't wakened him, when he noticed a piece of paper by the bed. The paper said, "It is 5:00 AM. Wake up."

Key #13

Identifying the Right Timing for Discussions

"Yes, there's a right time and way for everything, even though, unfortunately, we miss it for the most part." (Ecclesiastes 8:6 MSG)

Continuing on with the assertion that at the heart of healthy communication is respecting and honoring the other person or people involved in the discussion. Honoring the other person involves taking time to understand their mode of communication, keeping appropriate eye contact to assure interest in what they are saying and learning what motivates them (past and present events that have affected them). Part of this respect is taking time to discern not just what to say and how to say it, but also WHEN to say it.

Often children exuberantly greet their father as he enters the front door from a hard day at work. They cling to his leg and chatter one hundred miles an hour about who was not sharing, where the dog pooped and what they had for lunch. During this door side mayhem, if the child asks to go outside to play with their friend who lives next door, the father may say, "no," for reasons the child simply can't comprehend. Why would a reasonable parent deny such a request like going next door to ride bikes?

Scenarios like this one play out at 5:30 pm in doorways across America. Why? Not every working parent, but some parents who work outside of the home, need a half an hour or so to transition from work to home. Transition time is a vital part of the human experience. It is quite individual, in that one person may need ten minutes to transition from one activity to another, while another individual may need as long as a few hours to truly be present (mentally and emotionally).

Discussions during transition times are often difficult for the individual simply trying to get his or her footing on the "new terrain." In the hypothetical scenario mentioned previously, the father probably did not say, "No," because he didn't trust the child or feared for his safety. In all likelihood, he refused the request because it is our natural inclination to refrain from making important decisions haphazardly while we haven't had a chance to sit down and get ourselves together.

To hold the status quo (i.e. the child staying put) until the transition from work to home is successfully navigated will almost always be a person's first line of defense against the feeling of being overwhelmed. It is wise communicator know a person's transition period and respects that serious discussions and decision-making is better left to a time when the transition has been fully completed.

This practice can also assist you in the workplace. Approaching your employer for a raise at 8:04 am may not work well for you. Your employer also needs a transition time from home to work. Respecting that transition time will help you avoid the knee jerk, "No," from your boss when better results could be obtained by simply waiting until the home-to-work transition has been made, and your boss is settled at her desk, her morning emails are already answered, voice mails have already been attended to, and she is drinking her morning coffee.

The previous example also shows us another time to avoid discussion or decision-making. Most people do not like to be disturbed during their routine activities. Your fellow employees have morning rituals that have to transpire before any meaningful work can really get done. Maybe your spouse has an after work ritual. Don't talk to her until her panty hose are removed, her feet rubbed from wearing painful high heels, her hair let down and her face washed. Running in when she only has the left foot rubbed, and telling her all about the wonderful, albeit expensive, electronic gadget you think would be perfect for the den might not go as well as waiting until her hair is down, and she feels clean and fresh. In this way, refraining from our urges to talk, discuss, or debate in order to put the routines and transitions of the other person first is noble and respectful.

Let's face it, there are certain times within every day that, try as we may, we are just cranky and unapproachable. Is your spouse a night owl? Are you a person who loves to greet the sunrise with a smile? Take personal preferences into consideration when approaching your spouse for discussion. If your spouse works long hours and only gets four hours of sleep at night, be respectful not to have serious discussions at 6 am. Honoring your spouse in this way, will not only let him know how important he is to you, but will also give you a greater chance of having a successful conversation.

If you are a parent of a teenager, morning will also not be a great time to approach your lethargic youth. Maybe you are a night owl and spend hours at night processing your day's events in your mind. No matter how pressing a situation seems, wait until the next day to discuss your thoughts and concerns with your spouse. If you have to, write your concerns so you don't lose your thoughts. In this way, you satisfy the sense of urgency you feel about the matter, without disrespecting your spouse by waking them up from a dead sleep. Again, kindness will always be worth it. Always.

Be sure to consider the current life events affecting your spouse (or child). If work is particularly difficult, their responses may be short. Honor their stress level by saving the discussion for a more appropriate time, or at least don't blame them if the tone in their voice sounds stressed. Maybe your wife is particularly emotional this week. Take her emotional state into consideration. Can your conversation wait until she is in an emotional place to truly hear what you have to say?

If your teenage daughter is in the throes of a meltdown regarding the gardenias for the homecoming float coming later than expected, respect that it is going to affect the way she communicates and processes information. Even if any of these events seem trivial to you, look at them through the eyes of the other person. A forty-year-old man probably does not fret over gardenias, but a loving father can still care that it upsets his daughter. Parents can choose to approach their teens with serious discussions at times when they are not so emotionally charged.

Not only is this polite, but it is wise. If we want to be heard, it is prudent to choose to speak at a time when the ears of the listener are most open. If the ears of our spouse, employer, parent, or child are clogged with transition timing, stress, sleep, or routine, our voice will simply add to the noise that bombards them.

Waiting for appropriate times to begin discussions is a proactive way that we can set our voice apart from the other sounds of life. In addition, honoring the other person enough to restrain your desire to speak provides a healthy lesson in respect and meekness. Learning to put others first will pay off in the long run. Moreover, those around you are more likely to return your favor in kind and choose to approach you in your times of peace and stillness as well.

Key #14

*Conducting Regular
Family Meetings*

*"Fill up and complete my joy by living in harmony and being of the
same mind and one in purpose, having the same love, being in full accord
and of one harmonious mind and intention." (Philippians 2:2 AMP)*

In companies, regardless of their size, there are quarterly
or semi-quarterly meetings scheduled with the express
goal of getting everyone in the company, from secretary
to CEO, on the same page. This fosters trust and unity.
When individuals share time and knowledge, there is a
trust formed between them – they build a relationship.
Obviously, the more intimate the knowledge shared, the
more intimate the relationship that results. Regardless,
sharing knowledge enforces bonds of trust. Moreover,
sharing knowledge leads to a sense of respect and value. If
the CEO shares the financial state of the company with the
managers, the managers then feel respected and valued by
the CEO. This works well for the CEO, as those to whom
we give respect often feel inclined to return the respect
toward us.

Why should we put forth so much energy in maintaining
and fostering healthy lines of communication at work, but
assume that communication within our own family is just
going to evolve naturally? Many families have followed the

example of successful corporations and have conducted family meetings on a regular basis. The benefits to a family who meets regularly are as many, if not more, than the positive effects in a company.

Having regular family meetings is a proactive step against miscommunication and conflicts. Also, revisiting the family goals on a regular basis allows everyone to "refocus" and to stay on the same page. If the family's vision is no longer appropriate, having regular meetings would also allow for a restructuring of the vision statement so the family can set new goals.

Like the byproduct in a company, having regular family meetings fosters trust and respect. If the father shares how his stress at work affects the way he responds when he comes home in the evening, the children feel respected for having been privy to such information. Not directly or immediately, but eventually, this respect will be returned to their father. It is expressly difficult to disrespect someone who continually holds you in high regard. In this way, the parents can lead by example, sharing information and intimate details with their children (within reason of course). Hopefully, the children will be more likely to share openly with their parents in the future.

Furthermore, family meetings offer a comfortable setting to discuss concerns. A daughter may not feel comfortable telling her mom that she feels humiliated when her friends are over, but sitting around a table of honesty and safety just might open that door of communication. If ground rules for respect and honor are set in advance, the daughter knows that she can share without fearing a horrible consequence or negative response from her mother. If parents set safe boundaries to protect the sanctity of the things shared at the meetings, the gatherings that result will tend to be more open and intimate. Fear will no longer dictate what is said or unsaid. In this way, *"Perfect love casts out fear."* (1 John 4:18)

Thus, meeting regularly is a positive step toward guarding against miscommunication. Minor points of conflict can grow over time, but if they are addressed early will be washed away with open lines of communication and trust. Many times scheduling conflicts arise from simple lack of communication between those making the appointments or commitments. Discussing schedules once or twice a month can avoid the hurt feelings, missed engagements, or frantic afternoons driving to three different appointments that can all arise from being overbooked and under-organized. It also allows for open discussion about prioritizing. So many times we, as humans, assume we know the other person's motive. Thoughts like this lead to feeling that your engagement was "overridden," out of disregard for you. Talking about the events that will or will not be attended and WHY can allow feelings of resentment to be addressed before they have a chance to grow.

Setting regular times and constructing agreed-upon rules are vitally important to the effectiveness of a family meeting. Simply put, the gathering has to be a place of safety and freedom or the goal of good communication will be severely hindered if not completely lost. Setting it on a regular basis offers honor and respect to all who "attend." To further explain, setting the date for the meeting at every third Sunday prevents one family member feeling as if their plans are always preempted by a family meeting. This will avoid statements like these: "Well, we always have a family meeting during MY television programs. Why don't we ever have them during your news programs, Dad?"

Scheduling the meeting at a time and day everyone agrees on can avoid conflicts that can come even about the meeting itself! Also, having the meeting regardless of circumstance removes the guilt that can come if one of the children or a parent perceives that they themselves are the reason for having the meeting. For example, if a teenage boy is hanging out with the wrong crowd, the parents can discuss this openly with him at the next meeting. Neither parent needs to embarrass or anger the teen by saying, "Well, we are calling a family meeting to discuss your behavior." The meeting then is not a punishment. It is simply a gathering, nothing more.

Agreed upon rules will also provide a sense of safety. Much like the order at a corporate meeting, family gatherings need some ground rules. As a parent, consider listening to a concern then waiting at least 10 minutes to respond. This will guard against the instinct to immediately react and defend your actions. It will also provide a "buffer" for your child to disclose difficult information. This is especially important in your children's teen years. What they hide from you is ALWAYS worse than what they tell you. Allow them room to talk to you candidly, so as to minimize the details they keep inside themselves.

Cruel words are not to be tolerated. Cruelty will never lead to reconciliation. As agents of reconciliation, our goal is that our words and responses to the people we come in contact is met with kindness. (2 Corinthians 5:19) Another ground rule that you might want to consider is answering all questions. So many of us grew up with parents who said, "Because I said so," far more often than necessary. What this type of response leads to is the children's inability to make decisions outside of the parent's presence. If they don't know why or how your decision was arrived at, they have a harder time deducing correct behavior when dealing with new situations. If they ask a question, why not answer it? This is within reason. There are certainly questions that are too intimate or too mature to answer, but even then kindly declining to answer goes a lot farther than, "I said so."

Consider voting. Obviously, parents' votes veto children's votes. But on nonessential decisions, why not give the kids a say? The vacation spot is narrowed down to two places. You have three children. Let them break the tie. The two "winners" will feel trusted, and the one "naysayer" will still feel considered and heard. No, your children should not be allowed to vote ice cream in as the daily representative from the dairy food group. Important decisions can be discussed and voted on, instead of simply being forced on the children. The result, especially with parental veto power, can still be the same as it would have been had the parents made the decision without consulting the children. However, kids are more likely to view a situation positively if they at least they feel heard and valued in the decision making process.

Fostering these lines of communication, clearly displaying trust and respect and protecting the boundaries of sharing can get a family unified around a common goal. It is easy to lose sight of a family's commitment to share Jesus with the neighborhood in the hustle and bustle of everyday life. Family meetings can be a break from the chaos. After gathering, the family unit can refocus on the vision shared by the team. The prize will then take precedence over the momentary rough patches in the road.

Key #15

Controlling Your Emotions

*"Hot tempers start fights; a calm, cool spirit keeps
the peace." (Proverbs 15:18 MSG)*

There is a wise saying, "You never regret the angry words
you didn't say." This adage reminds us that angry words
seldom lead to resolution and often cause more harm than
good. There is probably not a human on the planet over the
age of 10 who hasn't regretted words they can never take
back. You can apologize for fierce or unkind words, but you
can never unsay them. The New Living Translation puts it
like this in Proverbs 21:23, *"Watch your tongue and keep your
mouth shut, and you will stay out of trouble."* How hard that
is! Our words have more power than we perceive, and this
is even more so for followers of Christ. Of course in times
of conflict, we should seek to have a pure heart and a gentle
spirit. However, if we find ourselves housing a less-than-
gentle spirit and a not-so-pure heart, we should strive to
keep our mouths shut.

James 3 even likens the tongue to a horse's bit or to the
rudder of a ship. Both the rudder and a bit are small, but
they can steer a huge vessel, like a boat or a horse. If our
earthly vessels (body, mind, and soul) don't want to go the
way of kindness, our tongues can be used to steer them in
that direction. However, it is far from easy. In fact, James

goes on to say that whoever can tame their tongue is perfect - in other words mature! Well, so we won't get it right every time. Controlling our speech when we are angry is still an honorable goal to strive toward, even if we fail sometimes.

So you and your spouse are both angry. You are in the throes of a hostile "discussion." You want, with every fiber of your being, to list why your husband is dead wrong in this situation. How do you restrain your emotions long enough to make clear and reasonable decisions? Perhaps, you could excuse yourself to the restroom. While you are there, prayer is your best line of defense. This "time out" will be a welcomed break from the ire that is spiraling in the room.

It is hard to find the right words when we are enraged, but taking time to breathe deeply and calm down will provide quite a bit of clarity. Remember emotions are physiological, too. Sit on the stool or the side of the tub and take 10 deep, slow breaths. Close your eyes don't focus on your current situation or the 18 reasons you deserve a better spouse. They say humming is another way to slow down your heart rate. Slowing the rate of your heart is a valuable technique in soothing your emotions. Once your heart rate has slowed, prayer is next on your agenda.

Let's discuss what prayer is NOT. Prayer is NOT asking God to reveal to your wife how petty she is being. Prayer is NOT asking God for a new spouse. It also doesn't include: asking for the upper hand in the argument, asking for a better strategy to persuade your spouse, nor is it begging God to make her apologize. Prayer is seeking God's heart on the matter.

When a messenger of the Lord came to Joshua before the Jericho wall came down, Joshua asked the "angel" is the on the Israelite's side or the opposing side. In Joshua 5:13-14, the commander of the Lord said, *"Neither one. I'm in the Lord's army."* Seeking the Lord's will on the matter will yield victory, but it will be the Lord's victory (not yours). God is not on your side or your spouse's side. Rest assured; God is on His own side. Your best line of defense or offense, for that matter, is to be on God's side. He always wins. Be prepared, however. God will only allow you to be victorious through humility and sacrifice.

So now you can emerge from the bathroom, calm and hearing the Lord's will in the matter. Perhaps you are still angry. Politely ask if you may have some additional time to calm down. This will allow both you and your spouse of take a break. If the situation really IS as important as you both say, surely it can wait an hour or two for clearer heads to prevail. If not, the situation isn't that important, and thus not worth fighting over in the first place.

Perhaps, your spouse won't let you "get away." There are times when dismissing yourself from the discussion might unearth some insecurity in your spouse. They may think that your anger will grow more intense if you are left alone to stew on it. Also, they may fear that you won't see their "side" of the issue and only ponder yours while you are taking a break. Don't simply walk off, leaving them to frantically follow you. Make pure and clean eye contact.

After eye contact is made, assure them in soft tones that you love them enough to want to only speak kindly to them. Promise that you will not brood on this while you are seeking time with the Lord. Assure them that this time will only make the discussion more productive and fulfilling. Taking time to reassure your spouse will allow this time of solitude to strengthen and calm them as well. Without stopping to show this kindness to a worried spouse, you are running the risk of the break itself becoming the topic of another argument.

Also, assure your spouse that their feelings are of value. For example, if a wife brings up a painful subject while riding in the car. The husband may think it would be better not to discuss it in front of the children, who are sitting in the back hanging on every word. Simply saying, "Can we talk about this later?" may lead to the wife feeling insignificant or less valuable than the children. Learning to validate your spouse's feelings can go a long way to getting that much needed break from the argument.

In the case mentioned above, maybe the husband could say something like, "Honey, I think that is so important. We need to get to the bottom of this right way. But, Jenny is hanging on every word, and she is going to repeat everything she hears. Can we find a time, soon, to talk this over?" Reassuring your spouse that the time of discussion will return soon, will avoid them fearing that the subject matter might be forgotten all together. It also acknowledges how hard it is for them to wait for the discussion. There is a measure of anxiety involved in holding a topic for an appropriate time. Promising your spouse that you will revisit the subject soon will lessen their anxiety in waiting.

What if the shoe is on the other foot? What if you notice that your husband is just too angry to listen or be productive? How do you ask him to take a step back? A general rule that will serve you well is: Don't tell anyone what you think they should do. Simple, right? Resist the urge to say, "Honey, you are getting out of hand and need to calm down." Regardless of how you choose to say it, if your spouse really is heightened emotionally they will always perceive your request for solitude as hostile or condescending.

Even the best intentions can be misread if someone is angry enough. Instead, ask if you can take a break. Say something like, "I really need a few moments to clear my head and calm down. This discussion is not getting anything accomplished. I would love to take a minute or two to regain composure." In wording it this way, or some similar way, you are not lying. The situation really is deteriorating, and your angry spouse really is no longer presenting himself or herself in an honoring light. Even though you are not lying, you are also not accusing or blaming your husband or your wife. In the end, does it really matter who needed the break?

Debating is best left for the courtroom or the talk show stage. In marriage, success has less to do with being right or wrong, guilty and innocent. It is more about being kind, responding in love, and resolving the issue at hand. If you are more worried about proving your point than hearing your spouse, shut up. If your spouse has put the issue at hand before you and your feelings, find a place of quiet to hear from the God. This is the path of reconciliation. In a marriage, we need to work out the issue together, yet keep the peace, and control our tongues. In the end, it is always better to be kind than right.

Key #16

Embracing Confrontation

"If a fellow believer hurts you, go and tell him—work it out between the two of you. If he listens, you've made a friend. If he won't listen, take one or two others along so that the presence of witnesses will keep things honest, and try again." (Matthew 18:15-16 MSG)

You may think of a happy couple as two people who never argue and who go through life without the need to confront each other. However, avoiding confrontation can be the kiss of death for a marriage.

Everyone knows a couple who lived together for years without fighting until they split up in an ugly divorce. While fighting, or discussing problems, may be upsetting and difficult to deal with, every couple needs to learn how to confront problems with each other and work through them so that unspoken concerns don't grow into anger or bitterness. When people bottle up their feelings, resentment will find a comfortable place to take root.

I am not suggesting that you scream and yell at each other and I'm definitely not condoning violent outbursts. What I am talking about is the need to talk to your spouse about issues that are on your mind. For example, let's say your spouse always takes off his/her clothes and leaves them lying around the bedroom. Every day you see them, you get a little more annoyed. Of course, this is a trivial example, but you see my point. Rather than dealing with this every day, you get mad.

Now let's look at a bigger problem. Perhaps one partner in a marriage is not working and is not actively seeking a job. The other person may be supportive, but over time the stress and pressure of being the sole bread winner may start to wear them down. Single income families work for some families, especially when there are children involved. But let's say that this family is suffering from the lack of income. Money is one of the biggest challenges faced in a marriage. The working spouse could bottle up resentment and continue to get up every morning and carry the burden. However, it is not fair for that spouse to continue nurturing anger without communicating the problem. When they finally blow up and perhaps wish to end the marriage, it would blindside their spouse.

When resentment and anger is harbored for a long time, the healing process can be harder. Of course, God can lead us in forgiveness and the healing of our relationships. But the longer a marriage falls into negative patterns, the more work it will take to change those patterns.

Unfortunately, many of us have grown up without a good example of how to positively confront loved ones. Many of us grew up in homes where problems were dealt with in anger and with yelling and negative words. Others grew up in homes where confrontation was avoided at all cost. Neither is the correct way to get positive results. If you want to talk about the clothes, you don't need to yell from the bedroom, "You slob! Get in here and clean up after yourself! What do you think I am, your maid?" Try waiting for an opportune moment (i.e. family meetings) and say something like this: "I feel frustrated when I walk into the bedroom every day and see your clothes lying around. I know it's not a big deal to you, but it would mean a lot to me if you would put them up." This way you let your spouse know what you need without laying guilt and blame on them.

I personally don't like confrontation. Therefore, when something is wrong, I shut down. But what I've learned is that in order for Lewis and I to stop having the same problems, I must let him know when I am hurt, I must let him know when he has done something or said something I do not like, and I must let him know when I need something from him. We cannot be afraid to talk to our own spouses about our feelings and we can't be afraid that confronting them may lead to an argument. What I've learned is that I cannot afford not to say anything. To have a successful marriage is to discuss, maybe even argue; yet resolve the issues and challenges we are facing.

If you are only communicating on a surface level (i.e. bills, children, work), something may be wrong. Again most of us don't like to argue and want peace in our relationships. However, we cannot be afraid to talk to our own spouses. Each time you and your spouse communicate, it should unite you more so than divide you as long as you're honoring and respecting one another's opinion. To have a solid marriage, it is not only important to learn how to communicate, but it is also just as important to learn how to communicate your problems before they become so big that you can't reconcile your differences. The remaining part of Matthew 18 states, *"I also tell you this: If two of you agree here on earth concerning anything you ask, my Father in heaven will do it for you. For where two or three gather together as my followers, I am there among them."* (verses 19-20)

Take the time to develop effective communication. The worst thing you can do is to act as though there is not a problem. Couples go months and years living with unforgiveness, anger, and resentment because of unresolved issues. So, how do we approach problem solving as married couples who want to work at the challenges/issues we are facing?

1. **Pray.** You must pray for your situation and for God to give you wisdom (James 5:16)

2. **Rely on the Holy Spirit.** The Holy Spirit will give you the right words to say and the self-control you need so that the discussion doesn't get out of control. (Matthew 10:19)

3. **Understand hard topics MUST be discussed.** Find the appropriate time and place. You may want to go to a restaurant where you both are relaxed, spending time together and where you can't yell at one another. (Proverbs 31:26)

4. **Listen carefully.** The bible says, for out of the abundance of the heart the mouth speaks; therefore, keep them talking until you fully understand their issue. (James 1:19)

5. **Change.** Change MUST occur to resolve the problem. You cannot do the same thing and expect different results. Discuss who will be responsible for what and make sure it's a win-win for both parties. (Matthew 18:19)

Again, we cannot be afraid to discuss anything with our spouses. However, if one refuses to talk, then the other spouse should pray and do their part while allowing God to do the rest.

Father, I pray that you will you teach me how to communicate more effectively with my spouse. Let the words of my mouth be acceptable to You and pleasant to others. Help me Holy Spirit to bridle my tongue that I will not say or do anything that will offend my spouse or others. Help me to discern the truth and speak the truth in love when conflicts arise. I thank you that my spouse and I can resolve our issues and improve how we communicate with one another because with You, all things are possible. In Jesus' name, AMEN

References

On your journey to achieving effective communication in your marriage, there are many resources you can use to encourage you and give you ideas. Consider taking a look at some of the following:

The Five Love Languages by Gary Chapman

Covenant Marriage: Building Communication & Intimacy by Gary D. Chapman

Cracking the Communication Code Workbook: The Secret to Speaking Your Mate's Language by Dr. Emerson Eggerichs

NOTE: These references were either recommended and/or considered the best in the field of effective communication and should not be seen as an endorsement by Jewell R. Powell.

This mini-book is part of the Marriage 101 Mini-Series by Jewell R. Powell, The Marriage Coach and author of "Marriage 101: Building a Life Together by Faith". Be sure to check out the other titles in the series - you deserve a 'happily ever after' marriage.:

Communication

Finance

Parenting

Sex & Intimacy

Marriage & Faith Journal

You can purchase a copy
at www.marriage101.us or call 301-743-5654